Bearded Dragons in Captivity

(With Notes on Lawson's Dragons and Frilled Dragons)

by Allen Repashy

Professional Breeders Series®

E C O

© 2006 by ECO Herpetological Publishing & Distribution.

ISBN 978-0-9767334-9-8

Copies available from:

ECO Herpetological Publishing & Distribution
915 Seymour Ave. Lansing, MI 48906 USA
telephone: 517.487.5595   fax: 517.371.2709
email: ecoorders@hotmail.com website: http://www.reptileshirts.com

T-Rex Products, Inc.
http://t-rexproducts.com

Zoo Book Sales
http://www.zoobooksales.com

LIVING ART publishing
http://www.livingartpublishing.com

Design and layout by Russ Gurley.
Cover design by Rafael Porrata.
Printed in China

Front Cover: An incredibly beautiful female Bearded Dragon. Animal and photo by Rick Millspaugh.
Back Cover: An adult male Frilled Dragon shows his famous attribute. Photo by Steve Swanson.

ACKNOWLEDGEMENTS

Thanks to those who supplied animals or photos for this project, including Michael Ready, Jill Griffith, Russ Gurley, Rick Millspaugh, Matthew Maribo, Steve Swanson, Jerry Fife, Bruce Delles, Kevin Dunne, Raymond Hoser, Kevin McCurley, Dean Wallace DVM, Bob Ashley, Ty Park, Alex Hue, and Mark and Kim Bell. A special thank you to Bob Mailloux at Sandfire Dragon Ranch. Your expertise and passion have motivated more dragon breeders than you will ever know. Your help and inspiration is much appreciated.

Contents

INTRODUCTION

A Kevin Dunne Sunburst dragon displaying its striking black beard. Photo by Michael Ready.

Australia is home to a wide variety of wild and wily herpetofauna. From top predators such as monitor lizards, or goannas, to the smallest tree-dwelling skinks, the reptiles of this often harsh land have adapted wonderfully to diverse habitats from the arid deserts of the southwest to the humid tropical forests of the northeast. Australia's dragons, members of the genera *Amphibolurus*, *Gonocephalus*, and *Pogona* are some of the most successful reptiles down under, having spread into most of the continent's habitats.

In the late 1980s, several species of Australian dragons arrived in reptile collections across the United States, mostly in southern California. The Coastal Dragon (*Pogona barbata*), The Inland Bearded Dragon (*Pogona vitticeps*), and Lawson's Dragons (*Pogona henrylawsoni*), which at the time were called Rankin's Dragons, were three that appeared and actually began breeding soon after their arrival. Early on, the large Coastal Dragons (*P. barbata*) fared poorly in captivity and its numbers declined so low that it nearly disappeared from captive breeding programs. The Inland Dragon (*P. vitticeps*), however, thrived in the southern California sunshine and began reproducing well. Numbers increased slowly and small breeding groups began to develop and spread slowly across the country. Initially, captive-hatched specimens fetched prices of $300 to $500 each. The smaller Lawson's Dragons mirrored not only the behavior, but also the fecundity of its larger cousin, and it also increased in numbers. But, due to its smaller clutch size, smaller body size, and less impressive physical attributes, it has received less of a following in the hobby.

Dragon habitat in Australia. Photo by Bob Ashley.

In the last ten years, the Inland Bearded Dragon has become an incredible herpetocultural success story. Like other popular pet species such as the Leopard Gecko, the Crested Gecko, the Ball Python, the Cornsnake, and a few others, it is now being bred in such numbers that it is being genetically manipulated for color, temperament, and even size. "Blood Red", "High Orange", "Peach", Tiger-striped", "Hypomelanistic", "Lemon Yellow", "Snow White", and other color morphs are being produced and sold.

The Bearded Dragon's spiny "beard" is presented in defensive displays and during courtship behavior. The male dragon's beard is usually more pronounced and darker than that of the female. Adult Bearded Dragons average 15" to 17" in length, though there are reports of large males reaching up to 23" (Mailloux, pers. com.). Bearded Dragons hatch out at 3" to 4" and grow quickly, many reaching sexual maturity as early as one year old. They tame down quickly and will often sit lazily on a keeper's lap or on a sunny

A beautiful orange dragon. Animal and photo by Matthew Maribo.

window sill of a watchful keeper's home, content that their place in the lives of reptile fanatics is enduring.

I hope that this book helps new keepers better care for their hardy and prolific pet dragons.

Allen Repashy
Repashy Reptiles

Chapter ONE: ANATOMY

The beard of the Inland Bearded Dragon, *P. vitticeps*, is one of its most recognizable features. Photo by Bob Ashley.

There are over 50 species of dragons in Australia. Though they range in size from small (*Tympanocryptis pinguicolla*) to quite large (*Pogona barbata*), they are all fairly similar physically, having rough, scaly skin, claws for climbing and digging, and clear, alert eyes. All dragons are diurnal, or active during the day.

Inland Bearded Dragons, *P. vitticeps*, have become one of the most successfully bred lizards in captivity. Through selective breeding and the occasional occurence of genetic mutations, many new and beautiful color morphs have been developed.

Body

Overall body length of hatchling Inland Bearded Dragons is approximately 3" to 4" and they weigh an average of 2 to 3 grams. As adults, Bearded Dragons attain a length of 18" to 24" and weigh

200 to 300 grams. The body is stocky and muscular, making them strong climbers and diggers. Dragons have large, triangle-shaped heads.

Bearded Dragons have four thick muscular legs with five toes on each foot, enabling them to be quick runners. At the end of each toe, a strong nail is attached which makes it possible for the Bearded Dragon to scramble over large rocks and to climb branches of trees.

Young Bearded Dragons use their sharp claws to climb on the decorations in their enclosure. Photo by Jill Griffith.

Dragons have a long, strong tail. Healthy dragons have a thick tail that is approximately twice the length of the body. Typically, dragons do not lose their tails easily. Those seen with missing tail tips are generally the victims of

A Bearded Dragon's nails are strong and sharp, giving it excellent climbing skills. Photo by Michael Ready.

bites from being crowded as youngsters. Also, adult males fight aggressively and may bite each others tails when attacking rivals. Unlike many lizards, when a dragon loses its tail, the missing portion does not grow back.

One of the most notable attributes of the Bearded Dragon is its beard. The large spiny protrusions from its throat are used as a signal to other dragons and predators. When threatened, the dragon will expand its beard and thrust it forward. In many dragons, the beard is dark and can be quite striking.

The purpose of the beard is clearly demonstrated in this irritated dragon. Photo by Jerry Fife.

Skin

Bearded Dragons have a skin covered with thick, rough scales, giving them an almost spiny appearance and texture. The skin on the ventral surface of the Bearded Dragon's body is more smooth to the touch. The skin is also very durable, giving dragons protection in nature from dehydration, from predators, and from the rough

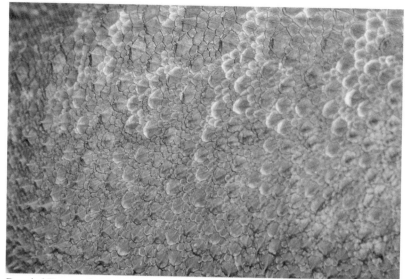

Bearded Dragons have rough, dry skin. Photo by Michael Ready.

rocky terrain.

The skin of Bearded Dragons, similar to other lizards, consists of two layers, the dermis and epidermis. As the Bearded Dragon grows, it will periodically shed the "old" outgrown skin to reveal a new brighter colored one. Just before shedding, the dragon's skin appears dull as it starts to loosen. When the old skin becomes completely separated from the new, the dragon will use its mouth to pull it off in patches and will eat the shed skin.

The process of swallowing a shed skin is called "ceratophagia" which means "horn-eating". Ceratophagia is possibly a defense mechanism for dragons. By eating the shed skin, no scent markers are left behind for potential predators to discover. Ingesting the skin also allows the Bearded Dragon to utilize beneficial nutrients contained in the shed skin.

Eyes

Bearded Dragons have large alert eyes that are stationary and located on the side of the head. Bearded Dragons have a well-developed sense of sight. Being diurnal, they rely on their ability to

The dragon's eyes are protected by scales. Photo by Michael Ready.

see well while searching for their food and scanning for moving insects and other small prey from their perches.

The irises of most Bearded Dragons are a beautiful variegated golden-brown color. Like other dragons, they have moveable eyelids that enable them to close their eyes while sleeping. For more protection, the eye is surrounded by a ring of small protruding scales.

Ears

Bearded Dragons have well-developed ears which give them a keen sense of hearing. With no external projections, the Bearded Dragons' ears are openings on either side of the head. A tympanic membrane, resembling an eardrum, covers the openings to protect the ear.

Smell and Taste

Bearded Dragons appear to also have a well-developed sense of smell and taste. In the wild, living in rough rocky terrain, these well-developed senses are essential to a dragon's search for food and for survival. Hatchling dragons eat small mealworms and crickets indicating their sense of smell and taste is already well-developed. The captive diet of crickets, mealworms and waxworms probably mirrors closely the diet Bearded Dragons eat in the wild.

Voice

Bearded Dragons are capable of making sounds but generally don't vocalize. However, hatchlings and adults will make a hissing sound when they feel threatened, startled, or scared. It is probably a defense mechanism to scare off possible predators.

Thermoregulation

Bearded Dragons are ectothermic which means they must rely on their environment to control the temperature of their bodies. Thermoregulation occurs when a dragon basks. This behavior allows a dragon to determine where the temperature is best suited to its needs at any particular time. Bearded Dragons absorb warmth and stock up energy during the daytime while they are basking. Bearded Dragons, like other animals that thermoregulate, use their food for growth and not for body warmth.

Chapter TWO: Choosing a Healthy Dragon

A beginning keeper should avoid very small dragons which are quite delicate. This one-month old animal is established and feeding well. Photo by Russ Gurley.

My first advice to new Bearded Dragon keepers is for them to avoid buying a very young dragon. No matter how cute they are and no matter what the seller tells you, hatchling and very small dragons are delicate, sensitive to traveling, and during this time, many die in captivity at the hands of novice keepers.

Is a Bearded Dragon Right For You?

Cage cleanliness, clean water, heat, and a variety of live foods are very important for the well-being of a pet Bearded Dragon. In addition, Bearded Dragons require sunlight or its approximation through UVB-emitting bulbs. Bearded Dragons require live food such as crickets, roaches, mealworms, waxworms, and even small mice, which will require trips to the local pet store or bait shop or will require you to have live insects shipped to your home from invertebrate feeder dealers. If a keeper is willing to provide these needs for his or her pet Bearded Dragon, they will become an interesting and exciting part of the family. For children wanting a reptile pet, Bearded Dragons, Crested Geckos, Leopard Geckos, Ball Pythons, and Cornsnakes are excellent choices.

Read, question, explore, and weigh your realistic abilities, physically, financially, and emotionally, and if you decide to enter the world of dragon keeping and breeding, this book should be helpful in beginning your journey.

Finding a Bearded Dragon

After choosing to keep a Bearded Dragon, and designing and preparing the proper enclosure, the next step is the search for a healthy animal.

Captive-hatched Specimens

Australia stopped exporting wildlife in the mid-1970s. This ban prompted the captive production of many Australian reptiles that have become established since these early days of herpetoculture. As with all wild-caught animals there have been problems with internal parasites, external parasites, and other health-related issues.

Captive-hatched Bearded Dragons are typically healthy, alert, and somewhat accustomed to human presence. With thoughtful care, they will eat well, grow quickly, and become wonderful pets.

Places to Find Captive-hatched Bearded Dragons

Shows and Expos

Reptile shows and expos are happening all over the country. In recent years there has been an increase in the number of captive-produced Bearded Dragons at these shows. Typically the specimens

---

Many of the best Bearded Dragon breeders can be found at the top reptile shows and expos in the country. Photo by Michael Ready.

offered at these shows are healthy, feeding well, and are excellent specimens to begin a dragon-keeping hobby. At these shows you get the rare opportunity to hand-pick the lizards you want to purchase and you often have the opportunity to speak with the breeder.

When having reptiles shipped to you, there is always the risk of receiving animals that are picked by someone who may not have your best interest at heart. Add to the savings of not having to pay shipping and the lack of stress placed on the animals from shipping and the shows and expos are an excellent opportunity to get some really nice dragons.

Bearded Dragon Breeders

Some keepers are fortunate to have a local dragon breeder near their home.

LASCO's Indoor Bearded Dragon breeding facility. Photo by Bob Ashley.

Bearded Dragons

Many of the top dragon breeders in the country are located in warm, sunny areas where dragons can be kept outdoors. Courtesy of Sandfire Dragon Ranch. Photo by Michael Ready.

Often, these breeders will welcome visitors (potential customers) to their facilities. In this situation, you get to see the breeder's facilities and see his or her animals. You might learn some of their tricks, glean some experience and helpful hints from them, and often gain a new friend or colleague with whom to share ideas and offspring. You can find these breeders through a local herp society, a reptile keeper at the local zoo, ads in a reptile magazine, or on the Internet.

Please keep in mind that many breeders do not allow visitors to visit their facilities or only allow those visitors who offer a long list of reputable references and lots of advanced planning for their visit.

The Internet

The Internet has developed into a huge source of live animals. There are several extensive websites that offer classified ad sections where one can buy animals and plants as well as cages, supplies, food, and more. There have unfortunately been occasional problems with unscrupulous, faceless dealers. When buying this way, one doesn't get to see the animals or the facilities, and many of these Internet dealers are simply buying and reselling animals. There are also concerns about shipping, even with overnight delivery services. There are Styrofoam-lined boxes, disposable heat packs, and most boxes can travel across the country in a day without a problem. We try to only ship and receive reptiles from April to October and are careful during cold nights in winter and hot days in summer.

If you are careful and inquisitive, these Internet dealers can be a good source for reptiles. When you contact dealers selling reptiles, ask plenty of questions. These people want to sell you a live animal and keep you as a future customer so they should be willing to spend a little extra time with you. Make sure they are charging a fair price by looking around at what these animals typically sell for in other ads and from other sources such as dealer price lists. Do your home-work. Most will be willing to send you photos of the specific animal in which you are interested. Find out about their packing and shipping techniques. Make sure they sound legal, logical, and safe for the animal. If the seller is rude or unwilling to answer your questions, move on and count your blessings. Typically, these deals end up being the ones you regret.

Pet and Specialty Stores

As interest grows, more and more pet stores are offering reptiles for sale. Not only are they offering reptiles for pets, but they are exhibiting healthy animals in proper and inspiring setups. Many are offering correct advice and stocking the best equip-ment and supplies for their cus-tomers.

A beautiful dragon and lizard display. Courtesy of Leaping Lizards. Photo by Jill Griffith.

Bearded Dragons

The best pet stores are offering a selection of supplies and cage decorations for a wide range of reptiles. Courtesy of Zoo Creatures. Photo by Kevin McCurley.

Now, with the increased emphasis on the true needs of reptiles, shops are installing larger enclosures with inspired setups. They are using better food and many are even offering veterinary services to properly care for reptiles before or during sales times.

Though many continue to get a bad rap, these shops are literally the front line in our crusade to educate the general public about reptiles. As the first stop for most people searching for a pet reptile, pet shops have the unique ability to inspire a beginning keeper's first creative ideas and to offer proper procedures for setting up and caring for animals.

Choosing a Specific Dragon

When you discover a Bearded Dragon that you are interested in purchasing, begin by checking out the dragon's enclosure. If there is a water dish in the enclosure, check the water. It should be clean and free of dead insects and feces. If other reptiles from different parts of the world are kept in with the Bearded Dragons, especially wild-caught specimens, we suggest you don't buy any.

Ask about the dragon that has caught your eye. Was it bred by the person you are talking to? Was it bred locally? What's it been through over the last few days?

Pick up the dragon: It should be alert and active.

Attentive care before your purchase is important, especially for younger dragons. Photo by Jill Griffith.

Check its weight: It should have a fullness to the base of its tail and its back legs.

Check its strength: It should push off of your fingers with force.

Check its skin: There should be no noticeable bumps, lumps, or asymmetry to its body. There should be no lesions, sores, or unusual discolored patches.

Check its eyes: They should be open, clear, and alert.

Check its nostrils: The nostrils should be open and free from any bubbles, discharge, or stuck substrate.

Check its mouth: The mouth should be free from injuries, irregularities, or lumps.

Pet stores should offer their dragons large enclosures that provide exercise, heat, and a varied diet. Photo by Jill Griffith.

Check its vent: Its cloacal opening (vent) should be free of any discharge or lumps.

Check its tail: It should be full and flexible with no crooks, bends, or missing pieces (unless you are aware that this missing tip will not grow back).

Ask about any guarantee the seller might offer. Is this guarantee offered in writing? Remember, you are often stuck with your decision with no possibility of a refund. In fairness, the seller can't know your home or the care you will offer and so can only guarantee the dragon's current health.

Newly acquired Bearded Dragons should be allowed to get acclimated to their new enclosures and should be feeding well for at least a couple of weeks before a keeper attempts to handle them. Once acclimated, Bearded Dragons will typically accept short periods of handling and even hand-feeding. All children should be supervised and instructed on careful handling procedures. A handler should sit in

A healthy baby Bearded Dragon may be shy but should be strong and alert. Photo by Russ Gurley.

the floor when handling their reptile pet. In case the dragon jumps or falls, it will probably not receive any serious harm from a shorter distance. As with all reptile pets, anyone who handles the reptile should be sure to wash his or her hands after handling.

Chapter THREE: The Enclosure

Enclosures for bearded dragons should offer plenty of climbing areas and shelters and access to clean water. Photo by Jill Griffith.

Bearded Dragons thrive in a variety of enclosures as long as their basic needs are met. We feel that glass terrariums make excellent enclosures for keeping Bearded Dragons indoors.

Terrariums

Glass terrariums can be wonderful enclosures for Bearded Dragons. We suggest a 20-gallon long aquarium (20"l x 12"w x 12"h) for up to three small Bearded Dragons. As they grow, they will of course need larger enclosures. Adult Bearded Dragons will require at least a 60- to 75-gallon aquarium (48"l x 18"w x 18"h). Typically aquariums are relatively inexpensive, available in a variety of sizes, and look nice when set up in a special part of a keeper's home. Secure and sturdy screen tops are available for these glass terrariums and are usually easy to find at local pet stores. Custom built enclosures are also popular and can be built inexpensively in a variety of sizes. Remember: Bigger is better.

Substrate

There is a growing movement in herpetoculture for the establishment of creative and elaborate naturalistic vivaria for reptiles. The business of selling driftwood, moss,

Enclosures, especially those for small dragons can be simple as long as the basics are provided. Photo by Russ Gurley.

misting systems, colorful sand, and supplies is thriving. Substrates are an important addition to the look of a naturalistic setup. There is some concern about Bearded Dragons ingesting sand as they pounce on crickets that wander their enclosure. Many keepers are using new "digestible" sand products such as T-Rex's Calci-Sand®. They are not only safe to use with most reptiles, they can provide keeper's a beautiful and realistic substrate, closely matching the red desert sands of western Australia.

We do believe that young dragons are easier kept on paper towel substrate. It is easy to clean, inexpensive, and prevents the young dragons that are just "finding their feet" in attacking prey from ingesting harmful amounts of sand. We do not use newspaper or reptile "carpet" as substrates. Also, we do not use aquarium or pea gravel because it could certainly cause problems if ingested. We do not use cypress mulch or pine shavings as cage substrates because they can hold excess moisture and they can also cause problems if eaten.

Cage Decorations

There is no doubt that the addition of driftwood, cork bark, stable rock piles, and other cage decorations is important in keeping captive

The proper setup for housing bearded dragons properly can be expensive but will provide years of fascination. Photo by Jill Griffith.

dragons healthy and stimulated. These decorations will provide both basking areas and areas for dragons to hide, to rest, and to sleep. If you collect branches and other decorations from nature, be sure that they come from an area that is not sprayed with pesticides and that they are non-toxic. (Check the list in this book and on the Internet for many sites with lists of poisonous and toxic species of plants to avoid.) Rocks and stones can be sterilized in a light bleach solution (one part bleach to five parts water) and then scrubbed with a soap-filled sponge and rinsed thoroughly before they are added to the Bearded Dragon enclosure.

Heating and Lighting

Obviously, a reptile from a hot, sunny environment is going to require plenty of environmental heat in its enclosure. In nature, reptiles move between hot, sunny areas and cooler, shaded areas to regulate their body temperature. A Bearded Dragon's enclosure should provide them with the ability to act out this thermoregulatory behavior by having a hot end and a cooler end. Add a hot spot over one end (100° to 120° F) to serve as the basking area and add some shelter at the other end so that a captive dragon can remove itself from the heat. This is the reason that 20-gallon long terrariums and other longer profile enclosures work much better for pet dragons. The basking spot should reach temperatures of 100° to 120° F, which can be provided by an overhead lamp in an aluminum clip-on hood. We use T-Rex UVB-Heat® bulbs that emit both UVB rays and heat. These bulbs must be mounted in a ceramic fixture on a sturdy screen top (or hanging just overhead) as they get very hot. The UVB is important and allows diurnal captive reptiles to produce Vitamin

There are a variety of heating pads on the market. These can help increase the ambient temperature of a Bearded Dragon enclosure when needed. Courtesy of Zoo Creatures.

D3 which in turn allows them to properly absorb the calcium they need to form healthy bones and to have healthy, working muscles. In cooler areas or during winter months, a keeper can add a heat source under the enclosure in the form of a reptile heat mat. The goal for a keeper should be to keep the entire enclosure in the 78° to 82° F range and to keep the hot spot in the 100° to 120° F.

Note: The temperature of this hot spot may seem very hot. Remember, however, that Bearded Dragons are desert-dwelling animals and they require a great deal of heat to get going in the morning. On a trip to Australia, I saw a Bearded Dragon basking. It quickly scurried away when we approached. Out of curiosity, I shot my temp gun at the rock and it registered an amazing 140° F! With a very hot basking area, a dragon can move into the heat and warm up very quickly and is able to get active more quickly. Cooler basking areas will work, but a dragon will take a great deal more time to warm up and reap the benefits of the heat.

* Be sure not to put glass terrariums outdoors on sunny days. They will heat up to dangerous levels very quickly, killing your pet.

Outdoor Enclosures

Some keepers in warmer parts of the world will be able to keep their Bearded Dragons outdoors for all or part of their lives. Outdoor enclosures in sunny areas provide the ultimate environment for your dragons. Be sure that you provide outdoor enclosures with secure screen covers that allow sunlight in and keep predators out. If you are unable to keep your dragons outside all the time, most breeders feel that 30 minutes of natural sunlight every few days will be enough to enhance coloration and to provide for excellent growth of captive dragons.

Chapter FOUR: Feeding

Bearded Dragons feed on a wide variety of invertebrate prey. Photo by Michael Ready.

Feeding captive Bearded Dragons is simple and straightforward. They are going to need a varied diet consisting of live prey: Crickets, roaches, mealworms, waxworms, and occasionally pink mice can be offered. In addition, they will feed on a variety of shredded greens and vegetables once or twice a week.

A keeper should provide his or her animals with the best possible nutrition. Gut-loading of crickets, roaches, and mealworms with healthy food is an important part of feeding your reptile pets. By feeding (gut-loading) your prey items a healthy diet, this nutrition is transferred to your animals.

We feel that small dragons should be fed insects every day and they should be fed finely shredded greens one or two times a week. We typically feed our young dragons small crickets every day and add a small mealworm every two or three days and a wax worm once every couple of weeks. We feel that small insects and small meals are best and there is the belief that large meals and feeding insects that are too large for the dragon can cause leg paralysis, choking, and even death.

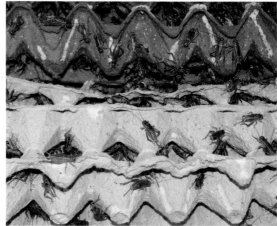

Gut-loading of crickets, roaches, and mealworms with healthy food is an important part of feeding your dragons. Photo by Russ Gurley.

As they grow, they can be fed larger insects, larger amounts less often, and their intake of shredded greens and vegetables can be increased to three to four times a week. Hibiscus leaves and flowers and rose petals are wonderful treats for your dragons.

Supplementation

Depending on the type of supplements you use, there are a variety of regimens to use with your dragons.

For most commercial calcium and vitamin mixes, feeder insects should be dusted every third or fourth feeding. We often reduce supplementation

Salads are an important part of the varied diets of captive dragons. Photo by Jill Griffith.

Most dragons will enjoy occasional additions of fruit to their diet. Photo by Jill Griffith.

Edible Garden and Flower Bed Plants

Amaranthus	Chives	Fennel	Rosemary
Apples	Cilantro	Fuchsias	Roses
Artichoke	Mint	Geranium	Snow Peas
Asparagus	Mulberry leaves	Gourds	Squash
Basil	Nasturtiums	Guava	Strawberries
Bush beans	Clover	Kale	Sweet Potatoes
Burnet	Corn	Leeks	Swiss chard
Cabbage	Cucumbers	Lettuce	Thyme
Calendula	Daffodil	Pansies	Tomatoes
Cantaloupe	Dandelion	Parsley	Tropical hibiscus
Carnations	Dill	Peaches	Violets
Carrots	Eggplant	Pears	Watermelons
Chickweed	Endive	Pumpkins	Zucchini

* A more thorough list of edible plants was printed by the California Turtle and Tortoise Club in **Tortuga Gazette 28(1): 6-7, January 1992** and is available on their website at **http://www.tortoise.org**. Another excellent list is available from Melissa Kaplan's Herp Care Collection website at **http://www.anapsid.org/resources/edible.html**.

to once a week for older dragons. (We feel that with a varied diet with plenty of fresh greens, such as collards, kale, mustard greens, romaine lettuce, and finely chopped vegetables such as yellow squash, zucchini, sweet potato, and carrots, the supplementation is not as important as most care sheets emphasize, especially when the dragons are offered UVB and occasional access to direct sunlight.) This is in an ideal situation. (When dragons are fed dusted feeder insects and a diet that contains a wide range of different vegetables.) If a keeper only offers a salad of kale or romaine lettuce and rarely offers other greens or veggies, then the supplementation should be offered every other time on the feeder insects and two or three times a week on the salads.

T-Rex's Dragon Dust ICB® has been developed for daily use. All feeder insects can be dusted with this supplement daily. In addition, T-Rex's Dragon Dust VMF® is also a daily supplement. It can be sprinkled onto the salad each time you feed your dragons.

Females that are breeding and laying eggs should receive insects that are dusted with calcium and Vitamin D3 every day. In addition, their salads can have a sprinkle of supplementation each time. This will ensure that they receive plenty of calcium for producing good eggs and for replacing any calcium that they lose from their bones during this time.

Water

In nature, Bearded Dragons get their water from rainfall and when dew is licked off of plants. To simulate this in captivity, we typically let water drip into a dish in the enclosure. This dripping will stimulate drinking. We set up a simple system with a plastic drinking cup that has a perforated bottom. This cup is set on top of the cage's screen top. It is filled twice a week and the water drips slowly into a shallow dish in the cage below. The dripping water stimulates the dragons to approach and to drink.

We soak our dragons once a week in a shallow dish of room temperature water. This will work for a single dragon and is especially helpful when a collection reaches larger proportions. A weekly soak makes sure that each dragon gets some moisture and has a nice long drink in clean water.

Chapter FIVE: Breeding

As mentioned earlier, Bearded Dragons are some of the most prolific reptiles kept in captivity today. If kept healthy and in a clean, proper captive environment an adult pair of dragons will most likely begin breeding and producing viable eggs as they approach two years old.

Sexing:

Sexing very young Bearded Dragons is somewhat difficult, but determining sex in juveniles over the age of three months is relatively easy. By holding the dragon in the palm of your hand with its tail facing you, carefully lift the tail up over the back and examine the area just above (posterior to) the cloacal opening. In males, hemipenal bulges can be seen on each side of the tail. The bulging hemipenes will also be separated by an indentation in the center of the tail between the two hemipenes. The hemipenal bulges are absent in females and the

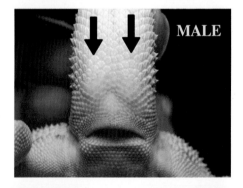

MALE

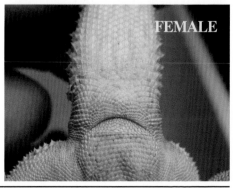

FEMALE

The hemipenal bulges are easily seen on the male dragon (top). These bulges are absent in the female (bottom). Photos by Alex Hue.

viewer will see only a slightly raised mound in this region. With some practice, this method works well even on dragons that are four to six weeks old.

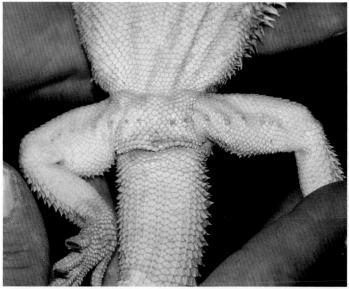

The broad hemipenal bulges are seen behind the vent of this adult male and the femoral pores are seen in front of the vent. Photo by Russ Gurley.

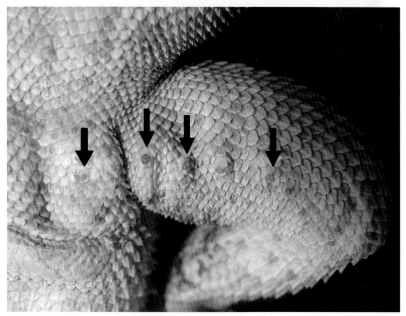

Detail of the femoral pores on an adult male Bearded Dragon. Photo by Alex Hue.

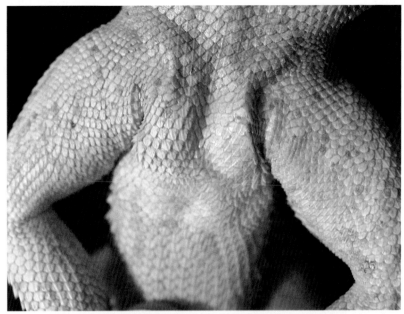

This adult female is missing the hemipenal bulges and the femoral pores are greatly reduced. Photo by Alex Hue.

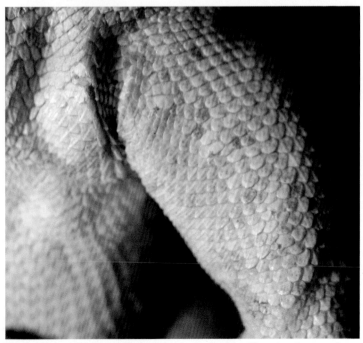

Detail of the underside of the back leg in the female. Note the absence of femoral pores. Photo by Alex Hue.

Breeding

Breeding Bearded Dragons is relatively simple. All that is needed is a healthy adult pair of dragons, an enclosure that is large enough to allow for breeding activity, and a suitable place for the female to lay her eggs. We recommend a resting period prior to putting an adult pair together. After feeding the dragons heavier than normal in the "spring" and "summer", a keeper should allow his or her dragons a cool, resting period for two months during the "winter".

We choose to separate our male and female dragons during this time.

Conditioning

From our experiences with insectivorous lizards, the best conditioning or resting period is provided by simply limiting the amount of food offered to the lizards. When feeder insects are limited, the lizards will move away from the daily routine of basking and will tend to rest in their shelters or seek out a part of the enclosure away from the heat. This self-regulation makes sense - if the lizard continues to bask and heat up, it will continue to burn calories. If food is scarce, it could lead to a dangerous situation. Therefore, cutting back on food is a first and important step in preparing Bearded Dragons for their resting period.

Also during this time, we cool the enclosure as well. We do this by removing any heat from under the tank and by changing the heat lamp overhead to a lower watt bulb (from a 100-watt T-Rex UVB-Heat® spot to a 40-watt incandescent bulb). We try to keep the enclosure (or the room it is located within) in the 65° to 68° F range.

After two months, the environmental heat is gradually returned to normal over a period of a week to ten days. Females are fed heavily once warmth is returned to normal. During this time, female dragons are fed feeder insects that have been dusted with a vitamin / calcium supplement each day. If kept individually, after a two week to month of feeding, the female is introduced into the male's enclosure. During this time, the males will begin to bob their heads and stomp the

A female Bearded Dragon, if given the opportunity, will dig a nest that is quite deep. Photo by Michael Ready.

As she lays her eggs, the female will often keep watch for any disturbances in her surroundings. Photo by Jerry Fife.

A female Bearded Dragon in the early stages of digging her nest. Photo by Bob Ashley.

substrate with their front feet. Courtship behavior includes the male chasing the female, biting her neck (and occasionally legs), and attempting to mount her. During this time, the male will often bite the fleshy skin at the base of the female's neck to immobilize her.

Bearded Dragon females will lay a clutch of 12 to 24 eggs (depending on the size of the female) every thirty to forty days when kept in a breeding enclosure with a male. They will typically lay three clutches in a season but may lay up to six clutches. As expected, the first clutches are larger and tend to have a higher rate of fertile eggs.

A laying area should be provided for females in the form of a pile of damp soil mixture, a cat litter pan full of damp sand and soil, or a pile of damp sand and soil in an outdoor enclosure. A female will dig a burrow (usually 8 to 16" deep) to deposit her eggs. Once she has laid the eggs and covered them, the eggs should be carefully excavated and placed in an incubation container.

Chapter SIX: Eggs and Incubation

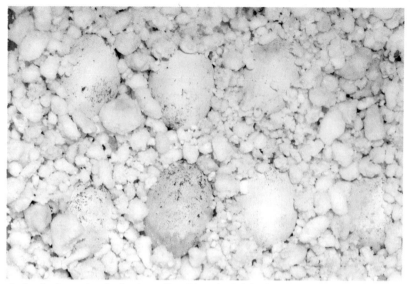

A clutch of eggs incubating in perlite. Photo by Michael Ready.

Eggs

Female Bearded Dragons will normally lay twelve to twenty-four eggs (depending on the size of the female) approximately 30 days after successful mating occurs.

Fertile Bearded Dragon eggs are leathery and white. They will remain leathery and will swell as the embryo inside grows.

Infertile eggs are usually smaller than normal eggs and are often yellow. They may be shriveled or may become shriveled in the first few days of incubation.

If the eggs look discolored, slightly dented, or infertile, do not discard them immediately as they may still produce healthy dragons. These eggs should be removed to a separate incubation container to prevent them from spreading any mold to other eggs. Also, these bad eggs may attract small gnats or flies into the incubator. The larvae of these flies may not only feed on the oozing infertile eggs but may also attack healthy eggs.

Incubation Medium

For Bearded Dragon eggs, there are two substrates recommended for use as the incubation medium. One is vermiculite, a type of heat-treated mica that absorbs and holds moisture. A second material is perlite, a type of volcanic glass that holds moisture well. Both vermiculite and perlite are sold at garden and nursery supply centers.

Some breeders incubate dragon eggs in a sand and peat moss mixture or even in potting soil. As long as the proper conditions are present, fertile Bearded Dragon eggs will usually hatch.

The dry substrate, whether vermiculite or perlite, or a mixture of the two, should be moistened with distilled or purified water. Too much moisture can cause the eggs to swell too much or to get moldy. (Too little moisture can cause the eggs to dry out.)

I suggest using a drier mix of incubation medium. Unlike the typical proportion of 1:1 by weight used for most reptile eggs, I use a mixture of 2 parts medium to 1 part water. This drier mix keeps the eggs from taking in too much water.

A breeder must be careful to watch the incubation container as this drier mix is less forgiving of mistakes.

A clutch of Bearded Dragon eggs hatching in a soil mixture. Photo by Jerry Fife.

Helpful Hint: The best way to maintain the proper humidity within the incubation container is to start by mixing the moist medium (2:1 ratio) and adding it to the incubation container. Once the eggs are placed in the container, weigh the entire setup on a digital scale. Then, each week remove the container from the incubator and weigh it on the scales. The weight loss for that week is the missing water that has evaporated. Slowly and carefully add enough purified or distilled water to bring the entire container back to the original weight. If you do this each week, the egg incubation container will remain at the safe humidity level throughout the incubation process.

When mixing the medium and water without digital scales, determining the proper moisture level must be done by feel. Add the water slowly and stir with your fingers frequently until the medium feels damp, but not overly wet. I suggest squeezing it tightly so that the medium clumps together well but does not drip water when it is squeezed. If it is too dry, add a little more water and if it is too damp, add more medium.

Incubation Container

Plastic shoebox or sandwich containers with lids make excellent incubation containers. Some breeders make small air holes for ventilation in the egg incubation containers and others do not. As long as you are careful and watch your eggs and their conditions closely, either system works well.

For ventilated boxes, place one or two holes in the sides or corners of the container. An inexpensive soldering iron or small drill can be used to make the holes. These ventilation holes should be small so the eggs or substrate will not dry out and the humidity level in the egg incubation container will remain fairly constant.

Even though the container has air holes for air ventilation, it is still necessary to remove the lid frequently. Be sure to replace the lid each time you remove it. This will let fresh air in and stale air out. If you are using a container without air holes, it is very important to remove the lid once or twice a week.

Most breeders will keep their individual clutches separate to offer geneticlally diverse offspring to their customers. Photo by Bob Ashley.

The egg incubation container, with the moistened substrate, should be ready a couple of days before the eggs are put inside. This allows time for the dry substrate to evenly absorb the water and for a keeper to monitor the humidity in the container to make sure it is correct.

Egg setup

Carefully remove the eggs from the laying site as soon as possible after the female has laid them. Before removing the eggs and placing them into the prepared incubation container, gently mark the top of each egg with an X using a Sharpie® or other marker.

Try not to rotate the eggs when moving them to the egg incubation container. The eggs should be positioned in the egg incubation container in as close to the same position that they were laid. Once the embryos start to develop, movement can cause structural damage within the egg, killing the embryo.

In the incubation container, make a depression in the medium with your thumb or finger. The egg will nestle into this depression. Leave a 1" space between each egg. This will allow room for air flow around the eggs. Also, this spacing will let the eggs expand as the embryo grows within.

Some breeders leave the eggs exposed while others completely cover the eggs with the medium. We place the eggs in the depression and push medium up around the sides of the eggs. Then, we place a 1/2 to 3/4" layer of medium over the tops of the eggs.

Remove infertile eggs. Each week, make a note of the incubation temperature, humidity within the incubation container, and the status of the eggs. These records will be useful for future breedings and are important in sharing your successes and failures with other breeders.

Incubation Time and Temperature

The ideal temperature range for incubating Bearded Dragon eggs is 82° to 86° F. At this temperature range, babies will hatch out at 65 to 70 days. Incubation times for Bearded Dragons range from 45 to as many as 90 days, depending on the incubation temperature. At lower temperatures, Bearded Dragons take more time to develop and thus hatch later. At higher temperatures, they develop faster, requiring less time to hatch. However, at the higher temperature, there is a greater risk of egg mortality.

Incubation – Incubator or Shelf

There are a wide range of commercial incubators available to dragon breepers. The inexpensive models work well as long as they are able to maintain the proper temperature without any problems. The

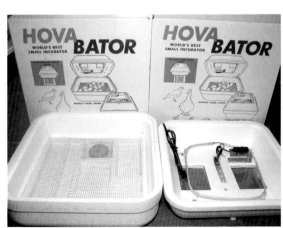

Inexpensive commercial incubators work well for hatching Bearded Dragons. Photo by Kevin McCurley.

Baby bearded dragons emerging from their eggs. Photo by Michael Ready.

models with built-in fans should not be used as they generate too much heat and will usually dry out the eggs very quickly. An accurate thermometer / hygrometer is a must in order to precisely calibrate the required temperature and humidity. We use a Taylor Thermo-Hygro®, Model 5368 to monitor both temperature and humidity.

For those with handyman skills, there are a variety of plans to build your own incubator in reptile books and on the Internet.

Many breeders do not use an incubator to incubate Bearded Dragon eggs. Instead, the incubation containers are placed on a shelf in a warm room or closet where the ambient temperature remains around 84° F. At this temperature, Bearded Dragon eggs will hatch out in 65 to 70 days.

Temperature-Dependent Sex Determination (TSD)

Temperature-dependent sexual determination (TSD) means the sex of the animal is determined by the egg incubation temperature

Baby Bearded Dragons will often rest during the process of emerging from their eggs. Photo by Jerry Fife.

and not by chromosomes at the time of fertilization. TSD is a unique, well-documented phenomenon occurring with turtles, crocodilians, and many lizards.

Though most breeders recognize that lower incubation temperatures produce mostly female dragons and higher temperatures produce mostly male dragons, much more work needs to be done to determine the finer points of TSD for Bearded Dragons.

Chapter SEVEN: Caring for Young Dragons

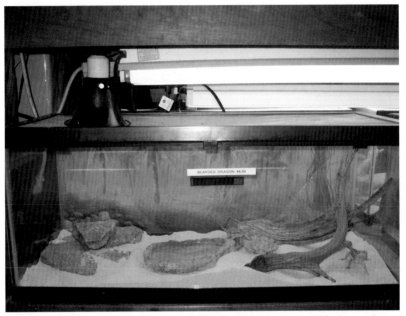

Even young Bearded Dragons should be offered a large enclosure with plenty of exercise areas and a thermal gradient. Photo by Jill Griffith.

We remove hatchling Bearded Dragons to their permanent enclosure after a day or two in the incubator. We set them up an enclosure for them in the days before hatching to make sure that we have all the pieces we need to maintain them successfully. We keep up to six small dragons in a 20-gallon long terrariums (20"l x 12"w x 12"h) or similarly sized enclosure. Once again, the length of this enclosure allows us to offer the young dragons a dry hot spot for basking and a cooler area at the other end in which they can escape the extreme heat.

The substrate in this hatchling enclosure can be paper towel. Paper towel is easy to clean and inexpensive. Care must be taken when removing the soiled paper towel, hiding spots, caves, branches, and wood. One must be careful to not set the decorations down on top of an unsuspecting baby dragon. We usually remove the babies to a plastic bucket while we are cleaning the enclosure and other times that might be hazardous to the delicate hatchlings.

It is important to offer a clutch of babies a lot of decorations in their enclosure. This allows smaller, less "outgoing" individuals to find a spot in which they feel secure.

As with the adult dragons, heat is provided from above by a heat lamp over the main basking area. For this size of enclosure, we typically use a

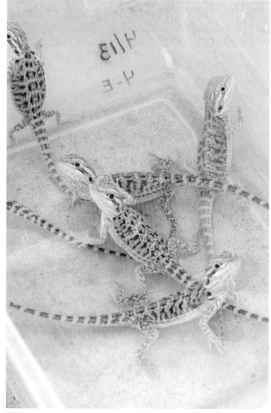

Young beardeds can be moved to a simple enclosure while their permanent enclosure is being cleaned. Photo by Michael Ready.

T-Rex UVB-Heat® 100-watt spot bulb in a ceramic clamp lamp to reach the high temperatures required for healthy basking (100° to 120° F). Care must be taken that this bulb rests on a screen top that is able to take the heat without melting or dangerously overheating. To regulate the temperature, these fixtures can be hung from the ceiling at a height of 18" or so from the floor of the enclosure. For most of our dragons, we also offer bright light and helpful UVB rays via a Zoomed ReptiSun 5.0® bulb or full-spectrum bulb in a fluorescent fixture mounted above the enclosure.

We begin offering small dragons their first meals at two to three days after hatching. We offer small (1/4") crickets first. Rarely will a baby dragon not be inspired to gobble up these small, active insects

Even young dragons will benefit from a salad of finely chopped greens. Photo by Jill Griffith.

when they come close. As mentioned earlier, we feel that smaller prey is better than larger prey. We choose to feed our young dragons small meals every day. After five or six weeks of eating small dusted crickets, we add a small mealworm or small waxworm to their meals once or twice a week. Mealworms that are small and that have recently shed their exoskeletons are the best choices as they are easier to digest. The waxworms are high in fat and provide little other nutrients, but they do add some variety to the diet of a small dragon. Finely shredded greens and vegetables are offered once or twice a week and any uneaten greens are removed the day following feeding. These salads include romaine lettuce, kale, endive, carrot tops, collard greens, carrots, squash, zucchini, apple, and others.

A high-quality vitamin / calcium supplement should be shaken onto crickets and onto the greens. This should happen once or twice a week for most commercial supplements. As mentioned earlier, T-Rex Cricket Dust ILF® and Dragon Dust ICB® have been developed for daily use. Check your choice of supplement's website to see what they recommend before using them.

No matter what type you choose, be sure to provide the supplementation that the fast-growing babies will require.

During the early weeks of having baby dragons, we do some shifting around of dragons as they grow. Any fast-growing animals are put together with larger animals and any runts are put together with other smaller dragons.

Watch for signs of aggression between baby dragons and remove any overly aggressive individuals (or the weaker ones)

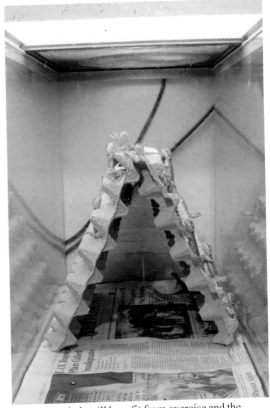

Young beardeds will benefit from exercise and the ability to spread out in their enclosure. Photo by Michael Ready.

to a separate enclosure to prevent serious injuries or deaths. Having a tank full of babies with missing toes and tails will not provide you with the reputation that you are striving for in the hobby.

Chapter EIGHT: Health

When dragons are cared for properly, they can be wonderful, long-term pets. This is Bubba, an 11-year old dragon owned by Rick Millspaugh.

While handling your Bearded Dragon or when it is removed from its enclosure during cleaning, it should be checked for signs of health-related problems. Young dragons should be checked for signs of respiratory problems or nutritional deficiencies as these are two of the most common causes of death in baby dragons.

Metabolic Bone Disease (MBD)

Metabolic bone disease is seen in young Bearded Dragons that are kept improperly or fed poor diets. Metabolic bone disease is a nutritional deficiency caused by an insufficient amount of calcium and inappropriate levels of Vitamin D3 in the diet. Dragons with MBD become weak and their bones will become spongy, especially the limbs and lower jaw. MBD also produces deformities in the fore-arms, legs, and spine. Twitching or tremors can occur, and they willusually lose their appetites. Once signs of MBD appear, reversal

The crippled hand of this female Bearded Dragon developed after it was raised on a poor diet with little or no vitamin / calcium supplementation. Photo by Russ Gurley.

of the condition is very difficult.

Good husbandry is the key to avoiding MBD. It is important to routinely "dust" feeder insects with T-Rex ICB Cricket Dust® or another high-quality calcium and vitamin/mineral supplement at every feeding. Some breeders will place a shallow dish of calcium in the enclosure so the dragons will have access to calcium at all times. The feeling is that dragons will lick the calcium when needed. In the early, rapid growth stages, sufficient calcium, vitamin, and mineral levels are critical factors for proper bone formation. Breeding female Bearded Dragons also need plenty of calcium and supplemental vitamins/minerals for proper calcification of the eggs.

Respiratory Issues

Respiratory problems are typically caused when dragons are maintained in an enclosure that is too cool or when they are chilled by a sudden drop in temperature combined with poor captive conditions and stress. A gaping mouth or bubbling nostrils are signs of respiratory problems. (When they are basking in extreme heat, dragons will often sit with their mouths open. This "venting" should not be confused with respiratory problems.)

Minor respiratory problems can often be corrected by the addition of proper heat. Moderate to severe cases will require a routine of antibiotics administered by a qualified veterinarian. We suggest that keepers make some telephone calls to local veterinarians <u>before</u> they experience problems to find a veterinarian that can competently treat reptiles.

The Association of Reptile and Amphibian Veterinarians (A.R.A.V.) is an organization that can help you find a veterinarian in your area. The A.R.A.V. is a non-profit international organization of veterinarians and herpetologists founded in 1991. Their goal is to improve reptilian and amphibian veterinary care and husbandry through education, exchange of ideas, and research. The Association of Reptilian and Amphibian Veterinarians (A.R.A.V.) promotes conservation and humane treatment of all reptilian and amphibian species through education, captive breeding, and habitat preservation. Check out www.arav.org for more information.

Eyes and Mouths

Bright, energetic eyes are signs of a healthy dragon. Dull, hazy eyes are signs of potential problems. Among the most common causes of eye-related problems are respiratory-related illnesses and improper diet.

Feet and Tails

If kept together, especially in a crowded situation, dragons can be aggressive and may bite each other's legs, heads, or tails. Check these areas for signs of injury. Minor injuries can usually be cleaned up with warm water and the application of an antibiotic cream such as Silvadene® or a triple antibiotic ointment such as Neosporin®. More serious injuries may necessitate a visit to a veterinarian.

If biting injuries occur, it is time to evaluate your dragon setup. Your dragons might be too cramped or you might need to feed them a

When they are crowded, a young Bearded Dragon's tail is usually the first casualty. Photo by Bob Ashley.

little more. You can add cage decorations such as additional basking spots and places for the bullied dragons to hide. Be curious and attentive. When you discover the problem, change the situation that is causing the problem.

In almost every situation where multiple dragons are kept, aggressive

Mouth and limb injuries are often seen in males who are kept together in colonies. Photo by Bob Ashley.

cagemates will grow more quickly and will begin to pick on animals that are smaller. If this is the case, the larger (or smaller) dragon should be set up in an enclosure by itself. Minor sores caused by biting will usually heal on their own if the dragon is isolated from others and is kept in a warm, clean enclosure with a dry, well-heated basking spot.

Eye infections are seen in dragons with injuries or severe nutritional deficiencies. Photo by Bob Ashley.

Swelling

Swelling is usually a symptom of an injury or an infection. We suggest you consult a veterinarian for any swelling, especially irregularities around the head of the dragon.

Coccidia

Coccidia are small protozoan parasites that occasionally appear in reptile collections, especially lizard collections. There is evidence that coccidia is often transmited to reptile collections in crickets that are raised in unsanitary conditions either at the suppliers, at pet stores, or at the keeper's facilities.

The intestinal lining of the lizard is invaded by the parasite, enabling reproduction to occur. Bearded Dragons infested with coccidia will stop eating, become dehydrated, lethargic, and anorexic. They may also develop a secondary bacterial infection. If a coccidia infection is suspected, a qualified reptile veterinarian should examine a fecal culture.

Coccidia parasites reproduce by means of oocysts, or eggs, which are released in fecal matter. The oocysts are the infective stage of coccidia. The oocysts must be ingested to invade another host to reproduce and complete their life cycle. When the fecal matter with the oocysts is deposited into the Bearded Dragon's enclosure, the dragon becomes the host again by

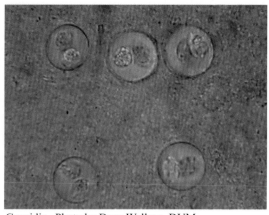

Coccidia. Photo by Dean Wallace, DVM.

reinfecting itself as well as any other dragons in the enclosure.

Quarantine any sick Bearded Dragons immediately, completely away from other animals in your collection. Clean and sanitize the animal's enclosure at least once a day or more. Also, have clean, sanitized enclosures ready and available at all times so transferring the sick lizard can be done easily with less chance of cross-contamination. When working with your Bearded Dragons, wash your hands frequently, especially if you are going from one enclosure to another. A strict regimen of cleanliness will help prevent spreading any diseases to healthy dragons or other animals in your collection.

Dragons and *Salmonella*

Note: I always tell people who approach me with concerns about *Salmonella* and reptiles to please not touch any of my reptiles after they have been touching raw chicken.

There continues to be much concern and much hype about pet reptiles and *Salmonella* bacteria. As reptiles become more popular as pets, some concerns over Salmonellosis infections continue to arise.

Most people today know that *Salmonella* bacteria are also found commonly in beef, chicken, chicken eggs, and some types of *Salmo-*

nella are even endemic in human populations in parts of the world. There is nonetheless the real possibility of small children and immuno-compromised people becoming infected by reptiles if their reptiles are kept in unclean conditions and if they do not follow common sense sanitary procedures when working with their animals.

* Recommendations for Preventing Transmission of Salmonella from Reptiles to Humans

1. Persons at increased risk for infection or serious complications of Salmonellosis (e.g., pregnant women, children younger than five years, and immuno-compromised persons such as persons with AIDS) should avoid contact with reptiles.

2. Reptiles should not be kept in child-care centers and may not be appropriate pets in households in which persons at increased risk for infection reside.

3. Veterinarians and pet store owners should provide information to potential purchasers and owners of reptiles about the increased risk of acquiring Salmonellosis from reptiles.

4. Veterinarians and operators of pet stores should advise reptile owners always to wash their hands after handling reptiles and reptile cages.

5. To prevent contamination of food-preparation areas (e.g., kitchens) and other selected sites, reptiles should be kept out of these areas—in particular, kitchen sinks should not be used to bathe reptiles or to wash reptile dishes, cages, or aquariums.

* *From Texas Agricultural Extension Service Newsletter, Texas A&M University System, Volume 11, Number 3, July-September 1995.*

NUTRITIONAL CONCERNS / Vitamin Deficiencies

Calcium deficiency

Metabolic bone disease is a major cause of death in young captive reptiles. An early warning sign of MBD is a reptile with weak limbs. By offering foods rich in calcium such as shredded romaine lettuce, kale, broccoli, and carrot tops, and by adding sprinkles of high-quality calcium supplements to food, this disfiguring and fatal condition can be prevented and even turned around if caught in the early stages.

Vitamin D3 deficiency

This condition usually develops from a lack of sunlight in captive conditions. Its symptoms include swollen mouths and limbs and lethargy. By allowing specimens access to plenty of sunlight and by adding fluorescent fixtures with high-quality UVB-emitting bulbs over

---

* SOME COMMON POISONOUS PLANTS

Avocado (leaves)	Impatiens	Pokeweed
Bird of Paradise	Iris	Potato (leaves)
Bottlebrush	Ivy	Pothos Ivy
Caladium	Jasmine	Privet
Calla Lilly	Larkspur	Rhododendron
Carnation	Lily of the Valley	Rhubarb
Chinese Lantern	Mesquite	Sage
Christmas Cactus	Milk Weed	Sago Palm
Chrysanthemum	Mistletoe	Schefflera
Clematis	Morning Glory	Snapdragon
Common Privet	Mushrooms (some wild species)	Sweet Pea
Cone Flower	Nandina	Sweet Potato
Daisy	Oak	Tomato (leaves)
Day Lily	Oleander	Tulip
Dieffenbachia	Peach (leaves, pit)	Verbena
Dogwood	Peony	Vinca
Dracaena	Periwinkle	Walnut (hulls)
Elephant Ear	Philodendron	Wisteria
English Ivy	Poinsettia	Yew
Eucalyptus	Poison Ivy	Yucca
Foxglove	Poison Oak	
Hemlock	Poison Sumac	

* This list was compiled from conversations with various turtle and tortoise keepers, from the reference below, and from personal experience. A very good list is available from the California Turtle and Tortoise Club's Poisonous Plant List printed in the **Tortuga Gazette 28(1): 8-10, January 1992** and found on their website at **www.tortoise.org**. Their list is based on the University of California Irvine's Regional Poison Center list of plants that are toxic or potentially toxic to humans

---

their indoor enclosures, this condition can be curtailed before it develops. By adding a vitamin powder that is rich in D3 to food items, this problem can be avoided. For captive Bearded Dragons kept indoors, add Vitamin D3 to their food and try to place them in direct sunlight as often as possible.

Poisoning

In outdoor enclosures, overlying trees and nearby plants often shed leaves and flowers into the pens. Bearded Dragons will usually eat this vegetation. If any of this foliage is toxic, problems including paralysis and death can occur. Mistletoe is a major culprit in some areas. *Rhododendron* and *Wisteria* cause problems in more tropical areas.

Fungus

The Bearded Dragon community has been alerted to an insidious yellow fungus has been responsible for the deaths of a growing number of captive dragons. Most of these dragons were initially being treated with an antibiotic prior to becoming infected with the fungus. It is felt by many keepers that the antibiotic used is not only

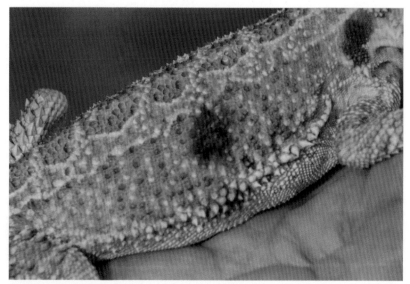

Fungus causes darkened spots which begin to deteriorate and will eventually kill the dragon. Photo by Bob Ashley.

killing the bad bacteria but also the good bacteria in their digestive systems. This allows a yellow fungus (thought to be a yeast that is normally in their digestive systems) to flourish and create massive infections.

This fungus not only causes massive damage internally, but is transferred to the outside of the dragon (with the feces) on the vent, arms, legs, belly, and other areas. This fungus is contagious and spreads to other dragons in the enclosure. Left untreated, this fungus destroys tissue and eventually kills the dragon.

In addition to treatment externally with antibiotic lotions, it is recommended that dragons that are receiving antibiotic treatment are also given probiotics to recharge their systems with the good bacteria that is wiped out during treatment.

For more information: http://groups.yahoo.com/group/ Pogona_Diseases/

Paralysis

A condition often seen by keepers who have a large collection of dragons is a sort of spastic hind leg problem or partial paralysis of the back legs. This condition is most often caused by feeding prey items that are too large for the dragon. This paralysis is usually seen the day after feeding and unfortunately is usually fatal.

Twitching and partial paralysis can also be signs of nutritional deficiencies and can be seen as an early sign of MBD.

Obesity

In captivity, many keepers overfeed their reptiles. An obese Bearded Dragon is recognized physically by having fat legs and an obese belly. Obese captive reptiles often experience liver and kidney problems related to fat deposition. This condition will greatly shorten the life of your dragon. This condition can be avoided by keeping your dragons in a warm, creative environment that is not cramped and by not feeding them too much.

Lawson's or Pygmy Dragons, *Pogona henrylawsoni,* in Captivity

A Lawson's Dragon photographed in nature in Queensland, Australia. Photo by Steve Swanson.

Lawson's Dragons (often referred to as Rankin's Dragons) are a small species of *Pogona* found in northeastern Australia. They are kept by a few dragon keepers but overall they have not been as popular as their larger cousins, *P. vitticeps*, the Inland Bearded Dragon. They have many appealing characteristics and will hopefully receive more attention in the future. One big bonus is that as adults, they reach only about 10" in total length. They are more delicate-looking than the Inland Bearded Dragon, with smaller heads and less pronounced beards. As with other dragons, they do well communally and a healthy pair of adults can reproduce well.

Housing

Small Lawson's Dragons will do well in a 20-gallon long aquarium (20"l x 12"w x 12"h) and an enclosure that is 36"l x 18"w x 18"h will house a pair or trio of adults of these smaller dragons. Lawson's like to climb so a keeper should design a creative enclosure for them to explore. Branches, driftwood, sturdy rock piles, and

A simple enclosure for one or two small Lawson's Dragons. Photo by Russ Gurley.

pieces of cork bark should be added. These exercise areas will not only keep the dragons stimulated, they will provide excellent basking areas for them. Substrate can be sand, a sand and peat mixture, or commercially available sand products. As with all dragons, access to a hot basking spot with plenty of UVB radiation is necessary.

A keeper should provide these dragons with a hot basking spot that is 100° F and a cooler end to the enclosure that remains around 80° F. A nighttime drop to 70° to 75° F is ideal. We recommend a day / night schedule of 12 hours light and 12 hours dark.

Feeding

Lawson's should be fed a wide variety of insect prey. Crickets, roaches, and mealworms are the best staple food for them. They will also eat small amounts of shredded vegetables and fruits. We feed insects to our Lawson's Dragons three to four times per week and greens and fruit only once per week. As with other dragons, a keeper should be careful to feed only small prey items. Baby dragons should be fed small meals more often (daily). We also are careful to feed small amounts of mealworms to small dragons and we try to pick out mostly soft mealworms that have just molted. The hard covering (chitin) of mealworms seem to cause some digestive stress to small dragons.

As with all reptile pets, do not feed insects caught outdoors. These may have been sprayed with pesticides and often carry a variety of parasites that may be transferred to your pet.

Young Lawson's Dragons and adult females that are breeding should be offered a sprinkle of calcium and Vitamin D3 on their salads or dusted onto their prey items. This will ensure that they show proper growth and that the bones of the egg-producing females stay strong.

Water

The Lawson's enclosure should include a large, shallow water dish. The dragons will drink from this bowl. The bowl should be cleaned and sterilized once a week or as needed when it becomes fouled with dead crickets or feces. We suggest soaking your Lawson's once a week in a tub with shallow, room temperature water.

Breeding

A healthy adult pair of Lawson's is quite easy to stimulate to mate and produce eggs. The pair should be cooled gradually over a two-week period down into the 65° to 68° F range. Their food intake is greatly reduced. This, and the cool temperatures will send them into a resting state under a shelter or curled up in the corner of their enclosure. Heat and UVB-emitting bulbs are removed and a small (40 watt) incandescent bulb is used instead of the stronger bulbs. The dragons are not fed during this time, but are given access to water.

This resting period should last from six to eight weeks. After this rest, the lights and heat-emitting bulbs are turned back on and the enclosure is warmed up over the next two to four weeks. When the

A healthy and alert pair of Lawson's Dragons, *P. henrylawsoni*. Photo by Michael Ready.

normal enclosure temperatures are reached, the dragons are fed and sprayed every couple of days. Within a couple of weeks, courtship behavior is seen and copulation can be observed nearly every day.

A keeper should follow the steps mentioned in the Bearded Dragon section of this book for obtaining eggs and incubating them.

Care of young Lawson's Dragons is identical to the care of other young Bearded Dragons. They can be raised together in large enclosures. They must not be crowded or underfed as they will begin to bite and eat each others' tails and toes.

Frilled Dragons, *Chlamydosaurus kingii,* in Captivity

One of the most impressive threat displays in the reptile world. Photo by Steve Swanson.

Frilled Dragons are one of the most intriguing lizards in the hobby of herpetoculture. Their spectacular frill and ability to run upright have seen them presented on a variety of nature documentaries featuring the most unusual reptiles on the planet. Though they have the reputation for being aggressive and hyperactive, they actually tame down in much the same way as Bearded Dragons and can make wonderful pets.

In Nature

Frilled Dragons live in Australia and New Guinea. They range in color (and slightly in body form) across their range and can be gray, dark brown, tan, and even dark orange with beautiful red, black, and light highlights depending on where they are found.

In their native habitats, Frilled Dragons are active, diurnal hunters. They feed on a wide range of invertebrate and small

Calm, captive-raised Frillies rarely display their frills. Photo by Bob Ashley.

vertebrate prey. They are quite arboreal and spend a great deal of time in trees near streams.

Choosing a Healthy Frilled Dragon

Frilled Dragons are still being imported in some numbers from Indonesian New Guinea. A keeper must keep in mind that these "farmed" animals are hatched on large farms in basically fenced off natural areas.

The eggs are collected and hatched and the hatchlings are sent to the pet trade around the world. Imports, like most wild-caught reptiles tend to be lower priced than captive-hatched animals. If a keeper decides to purchase an import there are a few things to consider.

External Parasites

An imported Frilled Dragon should be checked for external parasites, especially mites. These small black parasites will suck blood, can transmit disease, and can infect a keeper's other reptiles. They are most commonly found within the creases and folds of the dragon's frill. They are small, black, and active. They should be removed as quickly as possible using a combination of baths and safe mite removal sprays.

Internal Parasites

Though most of the farms that produce Frilled Dragons are well-run and relatively clean, there is a chance that your imported Frilled Dragon may arrive with internal parasites. Any reptiles that are fed in a farm situation and have access to both wild insects as food and are in locations near wild-caught animals may come into contact with the eggs of parasitic worms and can become infected. Any Frilled Dragon that is purchased as either farmed or of unknown origin, should have a fecal check done by a competent reptile veterinarian. If parasites are found, a round of safe wormer / antihelminth should be administered. Internal parasites will rob your pet of precious nutrition and combined with the stress of captivity can lead to the death of your pet quite quickly.

Dehydration

Imported animals often arrive dehydrated and stressed due to an extended period of holding before they are shipped to your local pet store. Once purchased, an animal should be soaked for a few hours in room temperature water in a shallow tub. We choose to use purified or RO water for our reptiles. Once rehydrated, they should be left alone for at least a week or more to allow them to get used to their new surroundings.

Captive-hatched

There are actually very few breeders working with Frilled Dragons. With a little research on-line, one can pretty well tell which dealers are offering babies that they have purchased and are reselling and which keepers are actually breeding and selling their own captive-hatched dragons. We suggest buying only captive-hatched dragons. Captive-hatched Frilled Dragons are usually more expensive than imported ones, but these dragons should be parasite-free, acclimated to human presence, and will typically make much better captives. This purchase will also support the work of a herpetoculturist working to produce these animals in captivity.

Captive-raised Frilled Dragons are often quite tame. Photo by Jill Griffith.

Sexing

Frilled Dragons are more difficult to sex at a smaller size than other dragons. In general, males will be larger as adults than females. They also tend to have much longer and broader heads and larger frills. They may also be more colorful, although this depends on the individual and its origin.

Captive Care

As with any reptile pet, it is advisable to design and establish an enclosure for your reptile before you purchase it. Frilled Dragons are going to require much larger cages than Bearded Dragons. We suggest that a single, small Frilled Dragon be started in a 29 to 30-gallon (36"l x 18"w x 18"h) terrarium. This long and tall cage will allow a keeper to establish a hot end and a cooler end. This will allow the dragon to bask under a heat lamp and will give it the other end to get out of the direct heat of the basking lamp. An enclosure temperature of 78° to 82° F with a basking site of 100° to 110° F is ideal.

Frilled Dragons require a large enclosure with a variety of supplies for heating, UVB-lights, and exercise areas. Photo by Jill Griffith.

A shelter such as a hiding place, sturdy rock pile, etc. should be set up at the cooler end and a branch or piece of driftwood can be placed below the heat lamp. This will let the dragon move toward the heat (and UVB rays) of the bulb and to move down the branch a ways to escape some of the heat when it has reached its desired temperature.

Adult Frilled Dragons will need an enclosure that measures at least 48"l x 24"w x 36"h. Enclosures for larger dragons should typically be vertically oriented. If one wants to breed his or her Frilleds, groups of adults can be housed in larger enclosures with a variety of shelters and basking areas. One male can be kept with two or three females as long as they are all about the same size and the females are large enough to breed and lay eggs successfully. Care must be taken that two males are not accidentally placed in the same enclosure. The fighting can quickly cause serious damage to one or both animals.

Substrate

Substrate choices for Frilled Dragon enclosures can include sterilized play sand, a sand and peat mixture or any of the coconut substrates available. We use a mixture of sand and peat moss for most of our larger, indoor enclosures. A keeper can keep young Frilled Dragons on paper towel. Paper towels are easy to clean and inexpensive and some keepers are concerned about young dragons eating sand when they grab feeder insects. We have not experienced this problem, but it is often mentioned on-line.

Cage Decorations

A keeper should strive to be as creative as possible when designing a Frilled Dragon's enclosure. He or she should add sturdy piles of stones, pieces of driftwood, grapevine, logs, and pieces of cork bark. These decorations should provide lots of places for the dragon to climb, to explore, to rest, and to bask. We often use sturdy live plants such as *Sanseveria* species with our dragons, but a keeper should know that these active reptiles will often damage plants in their enclosures as they move and jump about.

Heating and Lighting

As mentioned above, a keeper should establish a hot end and a cooler end to the Frilled Dragon enclosure. We recommend a hot end around 100° to 110° F and a cooler end that stays in the 78° to 82° F. A nighttime drop to 70° to 75° F is acceptable.

Frilled Dragons thrive under quality full-spectrum bulbs. We recommend T-Rex's Active UVB-heat® bulbs. These bulbs will produce the desired heat and will also deliver the UVB rays that are a must for the health of your dragons. We also place bright fluorescent and/or UVB-emitting bulbs in a shoplight fixture above all of our indoor dragon enclosures. ZooMed's Reptisun 5.0® bulbs or full-spectrum bulbs have proven very effective.

Of course, your dragons will benefit from being placed outside on sunny days. They absorb beneficial rays from direct sunlight. A keeper must be very careful when placing dragons outdoors. A secure enclosure that keeps predators out is a necessity. Keep in mind that local dogs and cats and raccoons are not the only predators of dragons. Keepers have lost dragons to ants, birds, and other wildlife.

Remember that glass enclosures heat up very quickly in the sunlight and they should not be used to house any reptiles outdoors.

Housing Young Dragons

Young Frilled Dragons can be kept in groups without too many problems, but as they get larger, males will need to be separated as they will begin fighting. As with other dragons, they will bite each other's tails and feet, often causing considerable damage. These damaged animals will be difficult for you to sell and they often remain stressed and fail to thrive.

Breeding groups of one male and three or four females are often set up by breeders. In these situations, males will aggressively bob their heads and show their frills to the females. In response, the females will rotate their heads in slow circles.

Feeding

Frilled dragons are insectivores and carnivores. Crickets, roaches, mealworms, and superworms should make up the basis of their diets. Small rodents are also enjoyed, but make sure the prey item is very small. As

Frilled Dragons benefit from a varied diet. Photo by Jill Griffith.

with other dragons, never feed your dragon prey items that are too large. We suggest ½ to ¾" crickets for small dragons, small roaches for all dragons, and very small pink mice for juvenile dragons and large pinks to very small fuzzies for adult Frilleds. It is easier to feed a few extra small prey items than to damage your dragon by feeding it prey items that are too large.

Some Frilled Dragons may eat a variety of greens including greenleaf lettuce, redleaf lettuce, collard greens, dandelion greens, and a variety of shredded vegetables and fruit. Our experience is that most Frilleds won't eat these salads, especially if they are well-fed with a variety of insects each week.

Supplementation

Dragons should be fed a healthy, varied diet of feeder insects dusted with a calcium and Vitamin D3 mix. This dusting can be offered at each feeding or only occasionally, depending on the supplement manufacturer's suggestions. Please read the labels carefully and do some research on what ones that the most successful breeders are using by searching websites and on-line forums. We use T-Rex Cricket Dust ILF® and VMF Dragon Dust®, which are supplements that can be used daily.

Female dragons receive added calcium supplementation during egg-laying season.

Water

A keeper should offer all dragons a shallow water dish. This water dish should be cleaned every couple of days or more if needed. Anytime an animal defecates in the bowl or if dead crickets are found in it, it should be changed. We suggest sterilizing all water and food dishes in a light bleach solution once a week.

We soak all of our dragons once a week in a tub with shallow, room temperature water. They seem to enjoy the soaking and this will often stimulate young and old dragons to drink.

Diseases and Health Concerns

We do not mix species. We do not keep Frilleds with Beardeds or any other species, no matter how similar their habitats and husbandry needs.

Please see the chapter on HEALTH in the Bearded Dragon section of this book for more information.

Breeding

Sexing

Obviously, the first step in setting up a Frilled Dragon breeding project is to make sure you have an adult male and an adult female. Sexual dimorphism (physical differences between the sexes) exists in Frilled Dragons. As adults, males tend to have a slightly broader head and more pronounced frills. To determine the sex of a Frilled Dragon, you must look at the underside of the dragon at the vent and base of the tail.

Males have hemipenal bulges located at the base of the tail, just behind the vent. Males also have enlarged preanal pores in an inverted V-shaped row just in front of the vent. In mature males, these pores will secrete a waxy substance.

Female Frilled Dragons do not have the hemipenal budges seen in the males. The area directly behind the vent is more of a smooth mound without the visual division. Females also have the V-shaped row of pores but they are small.

Sexual maturity of Frilled Dragons occurs between eighteen and twenty-four months of age. Breeding is possible at an earlier age but it is recommended to not start breeding female Frilled Dragons until they are two years old. Males will typically begin showing interest in breeding at one year old. Breeding females which are too small can cause stress and calcium loss which can lead to egg-binding. Egg-binding is a dangerous situation where a female is unable to lay her eggs. The eggs are retained in the reproductive system and can cause serious injury and death. Large females will usually produce more clutches with a higher percentage of viable eggs.

Mating

Like Bearded Dragons, Frilled Dragons, when healthy and sexually mature, and when set up in the proper enclosure with proper

Frilled Dragons benefit from direct sunlight and UVB-emitting bulbs indoors. Photo by Bob Ashley.

conditions, will usually simply begin breeding. Frilled Dragons can be bred as single pairs or in a group consisting of one male with two or three females. In a breeding group, a keeper must be absolutely sure that there is only one male. Multiple males will fight aggressively and can damage or even kill each other during their vicious battles. When keeping a breeding group of adults together, a very large enclosure is required.

During breeding, males tend to be aggressive toward the females. He will typically chase the female and grab her legs and neck, biting to immobilize her. This is normal breeding behavior for Frilled Dragons. If the bites break the skin of the female causing an open wound, the area should be cleaned with water and treated with an antibiotic such as Silvadene® or Neosporin®.

During breeding "season", a keeper should add a large egg-laying container inside the breeding enclosure. This container can be a large plastic tub and should be roughly 24"l x 12"w x 12"h. A hole that is 3-4" across should be cut in the tightly fitting lid. The size of the hole must be large enough for the female to easily crawl inside to lay her eggs. Fill the egg-laying container with a damp substrate such as sand, a sand and peat moss mixture, or vermiculite (or a mixture of all three). The substrate should be about 8-10" deep. This depth will allow the female to dig a hole, lay her eggs, and cover them with the substrate.

Many breeders will simply dump a pile of damp sand into the breeding enclosure, usually in one corner of the enclosure. This mound of sand will usually make an appealing egg-laying site for the female. This pile of sand can be reshaped each day if other dragons in the enclosure dig in it and move the sand around. If the female is reluctant to explore it as a laying area, construct a "cave" over the area. This will entice her and give her the idea that the laying area is secure and safe for laying.

Frilled Dragon females will lay a clutch of 12 to 18 eggs (depending on the size of the female) every thirty days when kept in a breeding enclosure with a male. They will typically lay three clutches in a season but may lay up to six clutches. As expected, the first clutches are larger and tend to have a higher rate of fertile eggs.

During egg-laying, Frilled Dragon females need an extra dose of calcium and vitamin supplement. Females need the extra calcium for producing egg shells and so their bodies won't take the needed calcium from their skeletal system. These females should be fed dusted crickets, roaches, mealworms, and even pink mice throughout the week.

After laying a clutch of eggs, the female should be given some time to recover from the stress of mating and producing and laying her eggs. Two to three months of "down time" should be enough for her to regain her weight and energy level, but different females recover differently. A keeper should keep close watch and decide when the female is ready to rejoin the breeding colony.

Prior to mating, a cooling down / low food period of four to eight weeks is recommended. This cooling period tends to imitate the natural situation in nature. For the cooling period, temperatures can be in the range of 70° to 72° F during the day and 65° to 68° F at night. During this time, dragons will typically hide in a shelter, cling tightly to one of the branches in their enclosure, or may simply curl up in a corner of the enclosure. They will remain in this resting state until the heat and light is reintroduced into their enclosures. Feeding is suspended during this time but a water bowl should always be available.

The arboreal nature is evident in this juvenile Frilled Dragon, photographed in nature in Proserpine, Queensland, Australia. Photo by Steve Swanson.

A thoughtful keeper will keep a notebook and keep breeding records. The data included should be when the breeding occured, when the eggs were laid, and incubation and hatching information. This information will be important for a breeder's customers and will help the breeder become a better and more consistent breeder.

THE FUTURE

Photo by Michael Ready.

The dragons of Australia and New Guinea have certainly taken their places as some of the hardiest and most exciting pet reptiles today. Bearded Dragons, Lawson's Dragons, and Frilled Dragons require somewhat larger enclosures than their smaller cousins, but their laidback personality and tough exterior have put them at the forefront for those wanting an exciting reptile pet. The beautiful coloration and striking black beards of Bearded Dragons are fascinating to many. The alert eyes and prehistoric frill of the Frilled Dragons fascinate even those keepers with a long history of keeping reptile pets.

For a reptile breeding program, dragons are prolific and they can produce clutches of healthy young for those keepers who offer them the proper captive care. In a breeding program, a keeper can breed for color, size, and even temperament.

When kept properly in large, creative enclosures, and when fed the correct diet, dragons are long-lived reptile pets that will provide years of educational experiences.

Bearded Dragons   71

PHOTO GALLERY

Red-headed pastel Bearded Dragons from Sandfire Dragon Ranch. Photo by Michael Ready.

A striking leucistic Bearded Dragon from Kevin Dunne. Photo by Michael Ready.

A beautiful red dragon. Photo and animal by Rick Millspaugh.

Sandfire Yellow from Sandfire Dragon Ranch. Photo by Michael Ready.

A Sandfire Pastel from Sandfire Dragon Ranch. Photo by Michael Ready.

A Blood dragon from Kevin Dunne. Photo by Michael Ready.

A Salmon Hypo from Kevin Dunne. Photo by Michael Ready.

A 10-year old German Giant Bearded Dragon. Photo by Michael Ready.

An Inland Bearded Dragon, photographed in the wilds of Eyre Peninsula, South Australia. Photo by Steve Swanson.

The Dwarf Bearded Dragon, *Pogona minor minor*, is a species not represented in U.S. breeding programs. This specimen was photographed in nature in Australia. Photo by Steve Swanson.

A defensive Frilled Dragon photographed in Proserpine, Queensland, Australia by Steve Swanson.

The Coastal Dragon, *P. barbata,* photographed in nature in Queensland, Australia. Photo by Steve Swanson.

SUGGESTED READING

BEARDED DRAGONS

Bartlett, R. D. and P. Bartlett. 2000. Bearded Dragons: Reptile Keeper's Guides Series. Barron's.

Cogger, H. G. 1992. *Reptiles and Amphibians of Australia.* Ralph Curtis Publishing.

de Vosjoli, P. and B. Mailloux. 1997. *General Care & Maintenance Of Bearded Dragons.* Herpetocultural Library. Advanced Vivarium Systems. Lakeside, CA.

de Vosjoli, P., R. Mailloux, and S. Donoghue. 2003. *Bearded Dragon Manual.* The Herpetocultural Library. Advanced Vivarium Systems. Lakeside, CA.

Green, D. and T. Larson. 2001. *Keeping Bearded Dragons.* Reptile Keepers Association, Gosford, NSW, Australia.

Greer, A. 1989. *The Biology and Evolution of Australian Lizards.* Surret Beaty and Sons, Ltd. Australia.

Mazorlig, T. 2000. Bearded Dragon: Success With A Reptile Pet Series. TFH publishing. Neptune, NJ.

Raftery, A. 2003. *Pet Owner's Guide to the Bearded Dragon.* Ringpress Books Limited. London, UK.

Weigel, J. 1988. *Care of Australian Reptiles in Captivity.* Reptile Keepers Association, Gosford, NSW, Australia.

Wilson, S. K. and Knowles, D. G. 1988. *Australia's Reptiles; A Photographic Reference to the Terrestrial Reptiles of Australia.* Collins, Sydney.

Zoffer, D. and T. Mazorlig. 1997. *The Guide To Owning A Bearded Dragon.* TFH publishing. Neptune, NJ.

FRILLED DRAGONS

Christian, K. A. and Bedford, G. S. 1995. Seasonal changes in thermoregulation by the frillneck lizard, *Chlamydosaurus kingii*, in tropical Australia. Ecology 76: 124-132.

Christian, K., Bedford, G. and Griffiths, A. 1995. Frillneck lizard morphology: comparisons between sexes and sites. J. Herpetol. 29: 576-583.

Christian, K. and Green, B. 1994. Seasonal energetics and water turnover of the frillneck lizard, *Chlamydosaurus kingii*, in the wet-dry tropics of Australia. Herpetologica 50: 274-281.

Christian, K. A., Griffiths, A. D. and Bedford, G. S. 1996. Physiological ecology of frillneck lizards in a seasonal tropical environment. Oecologia 106: 49-56.

Cogger, H. G. 1992. *Reptiles and Amphibians of Australia*. Ralph Curtis Publishing.

Ehmann, H. 1992. *Encyclopedia of Australian Animals*. Angus and Robertson, Sydney.

Griffiths, A. D. and Christian, K. A. 1996. Diet and habitat use of frillneck lizards in a seasonal tropical environment. Oecologia 106: 39-48.

Griffiths, A. D. and Christian, K. A. 1996. The effects of fire on the frillneck lizard (*Chlamydosaurus kingii*) in northern Australia. Aust. J. Ecol. 21: 386-398.

Shine, R. 1990. Function and evolution of the frill of the frillneck lizard, *Chlamydosaurus kingii* (Sauria: Agamidae). Biol. J. Linn. Soc. 4: 11-20.

Shine, R. and Lambeck, R. 1989. Ecology of frillneck lizards *Chlamydosaurus kingii* (Agamidae) in Tropical Australia. Aust. Wildl. Res. 16: 491-500.

Wilson, S. K. and Knowles, D. G. 1988. *Australia's Reptiles; A Photographic Reference to the Terrestrial Reptiles of Australia*. Collins, Sydney.